School

by David Mamet

A Samuel French Acting Edition

FOUNDED 1830

SAMUELFRENCH.COM

Copyright © 2010 by Daid Mamet

ALL RIGHTS RESERVED

CAUTION: Professionals and amateurs are hereby warned that *SCHOOL* is subject to a licensing fee. It is fully protected under the copyright laws of the United States of America, the British Commonwealth, including Canada, and all other countries of the Copyright Union. All rights, including professional, amateur, motion picture, recitation, lecturing, public reading, radio broadcasting, television and the rights of translation into foreign languages are strictly reserved. In its present form the play is dedicated to the reading public only.

The amateur and professional live stage performance rights to *SCHOOL* are controlled exclusively by Samuel French, Inc., and licensing arrangements and performance licenses must be secured well in advance of presentation. PLEASE NOTE that amateur licensing fees are set upon application in accordance with your producing circumstances. When applying for a licensing quotation and a performance license please give us the number of performances intended, dates of production, your seating capacity and admission fee. Licensing fees are payable one week before the opening performance of the play to Samuel French, Inc., at 45 W. 25th Street, New York, NY 10010.

Licensing fee of the required amount must be paid whether the play is presented for charity or gain and whether or not admission is charged.

Professional/Stock licensing fees quoted upon application to Samuel French, Inc.

For all other rights than those stipulated above, apply to: Abrams Artists Agency, 275 Seventh Avenue, 26th Floor, New York, NY 10001 Attn: Ron Gwiazda.

Particular emphasis is laid on the question of amateur or professional readings, permission and terms for which must be secured in writing from Samuel French, Inc.

Copying from this book in whole or in part is strictly forbidden by law, and the right of performance is not transferable.

Whenever the play is produced the following notice must appear on all programs, printing and advertising for the play: "Produced by special arrangement with Samuel French, Inc."

Due authorship credit must be given on all programs, printing and advertising for the play.

TALKBACK RESTRICTION

Until two (2) hours after the end of each performance of the Play, no presentation, performance or discussion of any type related to the Play, other than the Play as written by the Author, shall be conducted or authorized by the licensee in any venue. In the event of a violation of the Talkback Restriction by any licensee, such licensee's license shall be terminated, all sums paid by such licensee shall be retained, and all royalties due shall be paid. Furthermore, without limiting any other remedies, at law or in equity, such licensee shall pay to David Mamet the sum of Twenty Five Thousand Dollars ($25,000) for each single violation, as a reasonable and fair amount of liquidated damages to compensate David Mamet for any loss or damage resulting from each violation of the Talkback Restriction. By entering into an agreement for the Play, the parties hereto agree that such sum bears a reasonable and proximate relationship to the actual damages which David Mamet will suffer from each violation of the Talkback Restriction.

ISBN 978-0-573-69776-0   Printed in U.S.A.   #29232

> No one shall commit or authorize any act or omission by which the copyright of, or the right to copyright, this play may be impaired.

> No one shall make any changes in this play for the purpose of production.

> Publication of this play does not imply availability for performance. Both amateurs and professionals considering a production are strongly advised in their own interests to apply to Samuel French, Inc., for written permission before starting rehearsals, advertising, or booking a theatre.

> No part of this book may be reproduced, stored in a retrieval system, or transmitted in any form, by any means, now known or yet to be invented, including mechanical, electronic, photocopying, recording, videotaping, or otherwise, without the prior written permission of the publisher.

MUSIC USE NOTE

Licensees are solely responsible for obtaining formal written permission from copyright owners to use copyrighted music in the performance of this play and are strongly cautioned to do so. If no such permission is obtained by the licensee, then the licensee must use only original music that the licensee owns and controls. Licensees are solely responsible and liable for all music clearances and shall indemnify the copyright owners of the play and their licensing agent, Samuel French, Inc., against any costs, expenses, losses and liabilities arising from the use of music by licensees.

IMPORTANT BILLING AND CREDIT REQUIREMENTS

All producers of *SCHOOL* must give credit to the Author of the Play in all programs distributed in connection with performances of the Play, and in all instances in which the title of the Play appears for the purposes of advertising, publicizing or otherwise exploiting the Play and/or a production. The name of the Author *must* appear on a separate line on which no other name appears, immediately following the title and *must* appear in size of type not less than fifty percent of the size of the title type.

In addition the following credit *must* be given in all programs and publicity information distributed in association with this piece:

Originally Presented in New York by Atlantic Theatre Company, New York City, 2009

SCHOOL was first produced by the Atlantic Theater Company in place on September 30, 2009. The performance was directed by Neil Pepe, with sets by Takeshi Kata, costumes by Ilona Somogyi, lighting design by Chris Akerlind and sound design by Obadiah Eaves. The production stage manager was Gregory T. Livoti. The cast was as follows:

A ....John Pankow
B .... Rod McLachlan

CHARACTERS

A
B

SETTING

An office.

(Two people. An office)

A. The posters say "I will protect my planet…"

B. …yes.

A. …"by recycling paper."

(pause)

B. Yes.

A. The hall is full of them.

B. Yes.

A. There are hundreds of them.

B. No, there are more than that.

A. How many more?

B. Each child did one.

(pause)

That's why they're all different.

A. …they're all different.

B. …to express his or her…

A. "I will protect my planet by recycling paper."

B. Yes.

(pause)

A. Doesn't that use a lot of paper?

B. The posters are made on recycled paper.

A. The posters are made on recycled paper.

B. Yes. That was the students' idea.

A. *They* decided to use recycled paper.

B. For the *poster*?

A. Yes.

B. No. They *always* use recycled paper.

A. …*that's* the students' idea.

B. No. That's School Policy.

A. Well, then, what was the students' idea?

B. The text.

> *(pause)*

A. The *text*. "I will use recycled paper?"

B. Yes.

A. "I will save this planet by using recycled paper?"

B. Yes.

> *(pause)*
>
> *Using* it. Do you see?

A. No.

B. *Using* recycled paper. As, as, as…

A. …I…

B. …as an, not an "irony," but…

A. …alright..

B. As, they might say, as an "in *joke*."

A. …yes…

B. About the project *itself*.

> *(pause)*
>
> As a self-referential comment.
>
> *(pause)*

A. Why didn't they just save the paper?

B. There was no need to save the paper.

A. Why not?

B. Because it was recycled.

A. The "poster" paper was recycled.

B. Your *question* is: "can it be recycled *again*."

A. Yes. That's my question.

B. Of course.

A. "Of course it can."

B. Yes.

A. I…why "of course?"

B. It was recycled *before.*

A. But: I cannot conceive that it can be recycled *indefinitely.*

(pause)

Can it?

(pause)

Certainly, there must be some…"energy loss."

(pause)

Mustn't there?

B. Well, that's a question for the science teacher.

A. …yes…

B. I would think, I would think *nothing* can be recycled *indefinitely…*

A. …no.

B. As there must be *some* "energy loss."

A. How do they recycle paper?

B. "How do they recycle paper," they…

A. They take it and "pulp" it, do they not?

B. They pulp it.

A. So that:

B. …they take it and pulp it.

A. So: even if they reused *all* of the old paper, there would…

B. They would have to use new "energy," yes. In the "pulping process."

A. …they would have to use New Energy in the Pulping Process. *Such* energy having to have had to come from…from…

B. …uh…

A. From "somewhere."

B. That's right.

A. For example, uh…"coal."

B. Yes.

A. Or, "water-flowing-over-a-*dam.*

B. Hydroelectric…

A. Yes. Or…yes, or burning trees *themselves*, which is to say, the burning of "wood." Or…

B. Or "oil."

A. Or "oil," certainly, but from some *non-renewable resource*. To change the new thing. It is a principle of physics. That matter may not be created or destroyed.

B. Matter may not be destroyed?

A. No.

B. Why not?

   (pause)

A. You're joking.

B. No.

A. It is not a *prohibition*. It is a *description*.

B. I don't understand.

A. I'm not suggesting "matter may not be destroyed" is a *prohibition*, such as "This washroom is for students only." Or…

B. No, please, I understa…

A. Or "No smoking on school property."

B. No, please, I understand you.

A. …but a "*description* of the physical world." A term I would define as "the way things are."

B. Matter may not be destroyed.

A. No.

B. Then where does it go?

   (pause)

A. Where does it go "when?"

B. When we destroy it.

A. "When we destroy it."

B. Yes. As when we "burn" it. As when we burn paper. *You've* "burned paper."

A. It becomes ash.

B. But the *ash*…

A. Yes.

B. The *ash*. Must have less *volume*. Than the. The...

A. ...the?

B. The *paper*.

> *(pause)*
>
> Mustn't it?
>
> *(pause)*

A. What about the smoke?

B. The volume of the smoke and the ash equal the volume of the paper?

A. Matter may not be destroyed.

B. What about the firebombing of Dresden?

> *(pause)*
>
> Dresden was destroyed. Or if not, what happened to Dresden?

A. Dresden was destroyed.

B. Yes.

> *(pause)*
>
> And it wasn't even a Strategic Target.

A. Well. What difference if it was a strategic target or not. And, *and*...

B. I just...

A. AAAAND, *whether* or not it was a Strategic Target, would be a...

B. You're right.

A. Question.

B. You are correct.

A. For the History Teacher.

> *(pause)*

B. You're...WELL.

A. Yes.

B. But that just begs the question.

A. How so?

B. How so? *As*: the question is: what constitutes History?

A. *History…*

B. Yes.

A. As I understand it. Is, the Study of "What Happened."

   (pause)

B. According to whom.

A. According to whom?

B. Yes.

   (pause)

A. The Historians.

   (pause)

B. And have they never made an error?

A. The Historians. Being *Human*.

B. Yes. Of course.

A. Have "erred." The question is, *absent* historians. How would we know what had occurred.

B. I…

A. Even *if* they were in error.

B. If they were In Error, *then*.

A. …yes…

B. AT A MINIMUM. We would be misinformed.

   (pause)

A. That is correct.

B. With the attendant…

A. …yes, but, BUT. BUT. How would we know that we are misinformed?

   (pause)

   Which is to say, in what "way" would it affect our lives?

B. We would be acting upon faulty information.

A. Yes, but we would not "know" it. As if. For example: a man. Is caught in an unhappy marriage. BUT IS UNAWARE OF IT.

B. If it were unhappy, how could he be unaware?

A. If, for example. If:

   (pause)

B. If the sex were good.

A. Well, then, how could the marriage be unhappy.

B. IF, for example…

A. Yes…

B. The fellow.

   (pause)

A. "If The Sex Were Good" would that not, not "indicate," but "establish" it was an unhappy marriage?

B. A "Happy" marriage.

A. I beg your pardon. And, further, what "happens" to the paper. When it gets recycled?

B. They recycle it.

A. How?

B. *(pause)* I don't know.

   (pause)

   That would be Custodial Services.

A. Are they the Janitors?

B. Not anymore.

A. They're the janitors, yes?

B. That's right.

A. And *they* "recycle" the paper…?

B. They take it to the recyclers.

A. They are "tasked" with taking it to the recyclers.

B. Yes.

A. And we don't "know" what the recyclers do.

B. No.

   (pause)

A. Could we enquire?

B. Why?

A. So…

B. So we would "know"…

A. Yes.

B. Why would that be necessary?

A. Because. It *occurs* to me that, *perhaps*. A better Use of the Posters. Would be *to*: *Keep* them. And, for example, "Cut them up into little 'cards'," and use them for notepaper.

B. No, we…

A. For the secretaries.

B. No. We couldn't do that.

A. Why not?

B. You're kidding.

   (pause)

A. No.

B. You're not kidding?

A. No. I'm serious.

   (pause)

B. We…

A. "Cut up…"

B. Cut up. The work of *students*.

   (pause)

   We cut up the work of students.

A. Yes.

B. Based upon…? Based upon what?

   (pause)

   Based upon what criteria?

A. That it was hanging on the wall.

B. *(pause) Because* we'd have to…to destroy AND USE ALL of it.

A. For fear of…

B. That's right.

A. No. SO THAT. To *reuse* the, the…

B. "Work."

A. Could be said, not to be a sign of...

B. "Disrespect."

A. ...of disrespect. But...

B. ...yes.

(pause)

A. "An endorsement?"

B. No.

A. No, it could hardly be "an endorsement" to cut the, the...

B. Student's.

A. To cut up the student's work. ON THE OTHER HAND.

B. This is why, *this* is why I...

A. No, you're right. We...

B. Leave it to the Custodial Staff.

A. Let *them* take it to the recyclers.

B. Yes.

A. That's something that we can be proud of.

B. To the extent they do.

A. Well, do they take it to the recyclers or not?

B. When they have the time.

A. What do they do when they don't have the time?

B. We do not enquire as to the *specific* uses of their time. As long as the tasks are accomplished.

A. What if the tasks are not accomplished?

B. Well. The tasks will always be accomplished.

A. Be...?

B. Because they set the tasks.

A. The janitors set the tasks?

B. Well. To whom would you give that responsibility

A. They "set their own tasks."

B. Yes.

A. The "unions."

B. The "unions," who are made of *Janitors*. Set the Tasks for the Janitors. Which is to say, for the custodians.

A. And what is the *difference*? Between a strategic, and a non-strategic target?

(pause)

As we "won" the war.

B. Well, that's a narrow view.

A. A narrow view as its debatable if we won the war?

B. No, we "won" the war. Though, while not debatable, it is ironic. That the cars we drive. Are made by the nations we obliterated. That's ironic.

A. And I *wonder*. If child molesters. Should be forced to register.

B. How else would we know where they are?

A. Yes, but, dragging that chain. From one community, to the next. How could they re-start their lives?

B. No one can restart his or her life.

A. Why not? Which, you will see, is a philosophical question.

B. Then let it be answered by philosophers.

A. They're using *paper* – to *discourage* ideas, to *shame* those who use *paper*. And these "signs," for example: "This Washroom is for the Students ONLY. No Adults Allowed."

B. Yes. That *itself* uses paper.

A. And doesn't that "sexualize" the young?"

(pause)

I wonder about that crossing guard.

B. Which one?

A. You know.

B. …mmm.

A. *(pause)* You see, this is the problem of *command*.

B. Mm.

A. To say *nothing*. Is to risk, um
um…

B. Yes.

A. And become liable.

B. …not-if-we-didn't-know.

A. Not if we didn't know, indeed.

B. As we *don't* know.

A. *While*, on the other hand, to "act"…

B. Is to risk injustice.

A. AND legal action by the Union.

B. Not if it's true.

A. Well, curiously, *especially* if it's true.

B. Howso?

A. As preliminary DENIABLE discussions have led to the deniable suggesting that, were we to proceed, they might anonymously file charges against us for dereliction for not acting to remove an ongoing known menace.

(pause)

B. But how would they know that we knew?

A. We put up the sign.

B. *(sotto)* But I thought they *allowed* the sign.

A. The Janitors.

B. Yes.

A. They *suggested* the sign.

(pause)

I believed, at the time, it was a compromise. I see now it was a tactical ploy.

B. Those swine.

(pause)

A. Well. They're very political.

B. We could *bar* the crossing-guard-inquestion, from access to the campus.

A. The union won't allow it.

B. Why?

A. Unaccused, and unconvicted? It's a violation of his rights.

B. What about an "entrapment scheme?"

A. How would it work?

B. We take a *student*...

A. A "gay" student...?

B. *(sotto)* ...how do we know that they're "gay?"

A. *(sotto)* Oh *please*...

B. *(sotto)* Are we thinking about the same...

A. Well...

B. You know, I feel that *many* of these kids. Behave in a seductive and provocative way. Essentially, to torment the teachers.

A. ...um...

B. In effect, they're "cruising."

   (pause)

   Especially in the Lower School.

   (A sighs.)

   And, you turn around and "do" anything about it, and you spend the rest of your life in jail.

A. Not if it's not discovered.

B. Oh, it's all discovered. It all comes out. And, as I say, I wonder if that's not their *point*. The little *pigs*.

A. Well. I don't share your tastes, but I share your perception.

B. And I find their *dress* so provocative.

A. As who does not. *More* to the point: If we had a regulation, against making posters. We would save the paper, and the cost, both in material, and in worker-hours. D'you think the teachers would allow it?

B. That's all they *do* is make posters. That's all they *do*. That's all they *do*. One month to the next. What else do they *do*? For the love of God? These budding *Einsteins*.

A. And bombing, I feel, based on no personal "knowledge," but "intuitively," must *usually* be a mistake.

B. Howso?

A. As it must strengthen the resolve of the bombed.

B. Well. It might certainly do so.

A. Might? It certainly *must.* Imagine: crockery flying. The. The.

B. Accumulation.

A. The accumulation of *years*. Of brica-brac. Mementoes.

B. Yes, that's certainly true.

A. *Plaques* that one accrues.

B. Mm hmm.

A. For years of Service.

B. ...yes.

A. One has to *dust* them. But one doesn't want some foreign *swine*. Raining down ordnance upon one's *treasures*.

(pause)

And what about the ink?

B. The ink?

A. The *poster* ink. The *ink* came from somewhere. There was a cost for the *ink*. In energy. And resources.

B. But: If we did not expend resources...

A. Mmm...

B. In the poster. In the paper. In the ink...

A. Mmm hmm...

B. And even on the *sign*...

A. ...Alright.

B. ...how would we transmit information?

ABOUT THE AUTHOR

DAVID MAMET is a dramatist, director, novelist, poet, and essayist. He has written the screenplays for more than twenty films, including *Heist, Spartan, House of Games, The Spanish Prisoner, The Winslow Boy, Wag the Dog,* and *The Verdict.* His more than twenty plays include *Oleanna, The Cryptogram, Speed-the-Plow, American Buffalo, Sexual Perversity in Chicago,* and the Pulitzer Prize–winning *Glengarry Glen Ross.* Born in Chicago in 1947, Mamet has taught at the Yale School of Drama, New York University, and Goddard College, and he lectures at the Atlantic Theater Company, of which he is a founding member.

Also by
David Mamet...

American Buffalo
Bobby Gould in Hell
The Cherry Orchard
Dark Pony
The Dissappearance of the Jews
Dramatic Sketches and Monologues
The Duck Variations
Edmond
The Frog Prince
Glengarry Glen Ross
Goldberg Street
Keep Your Pantheon
Lakeboat
A Life in the Theatre
The Luftmensch
Mr. Happiness
The Old Neighborhood
November
The Poet and the Rent
Race
Reunion
The Sanctity of Marriage
The Shawl
Speed-the-Plow
Squirrels
The Water Engine
The Woods

Please visit our website **samuelfrench.com** for complete descriptions and licensing information.

OTHER TITLES AVAILABLE FROM SAMUEL FRENCH

RACE

David Mamet

Drama / 3m, 1f / Interior

Multiple Award-winning playwright/director David Mamet tackles America's most controversial topic in a provocative new tale of sex, guilt and bold accusations.

Two lawyers find themselves defending a wealthy white executive charged with raping a black woman. When a new legal assistant gets involved in the case, the opinions that boil beneath explode to the surface. When David Mamet turns the spotlight on what we think but can't say, dangerous truths are revealed, and no punches are spared.

"Scapel-edged intelligence!"
– *New York Times*

"Provocative and profane!"
– *NY-1*

"Mamet is most concerned with the power and treachery of language: a line of dialogue vital to the prosecution case is cynically rewritten by the defense. Mamet's larger contention is that attempts to create a more equal and tolerant society have made race an unsayable word…brilliantly contrives here a moment in which the single most taboo sexual expletive is ignored by an audience which then gasps at the word "black"…Mamet remains American theatre's most urgent five-letter word."
– *The Guardian*

"Intellectually salacious…Gripping…rapid-fire Mametian style… Mamet's new play argues, everything in America — and this play throws sex, rape, the law, employment and relationships into its 90 minutes of stage wrangling — is still about race."
– *Chcago Tribune*

"There is intrigue within intrigue, showing how personal prejudice and individual missteps govern the course of things…Mamet adroitly mixes comic darts with tragic arrows."
– *Bloomberg News*

SAMUELFRENCH.COM

OTHER TITLES AVAILABLE FROM SAMUEL FRENCH

NOVEMBER

David Mamet

Comedy / 4m, 1f

David Mamet's new Oval Office satire depicts one day in the life of a beleaguered American commander-in-chief.

It's November in a Presidential election year, and incumbent Charles Smith's chances for reelection are looking grim. Approval ratings are down, his money's running out, and nuclear war might be imminent. Though his staff has thrown in the towel and his wife has begun to prepare for her post-White House life, Chuck isn't ready to give up just yet. Amidst the biggest fight of his political career, the President has to find time to pardon a couple of turkeys — saving them from the slaughter before Thanksgiving — and this simple PR event inspires Smith to risk it all in attempt to win back public support. With Mamet's characteristic no-holds-barred style, *November* is a scathingly hilarious take on the state of America today and the lengths to which people will go to win.

"At once a barbarian, a bully, and an idiot ('I always felt that I'd do something memorable—I just assumed it'd be getting impeached,' he says), Smith brings oxygen to Mamet's rhetorical brilliance—so much that Mamet seems almost giddy with pleasure as he makes his cretinous creation squirm..."

"Broadway comedy is generally a testament to Twain's maxim that honesty is the best of all the lost arts. On the boulevard, laughter is meant to distract, not galvanize, to enchant, not disenchant. Into this weak hand, David Mamet has dealt an ace."
—*John Lahr, The New Yorker*

SAMUELFRENCH.COM

www.ingramcontent.com/pod-product-compliance
Lightning Source LLC
Chambersburg PA
CBHW070651300426
44111CB00013B/2367